BRUCE LE
CAUGHT ON CAMERA

Forword by Rick Baker

Bruce Lee (Chinese: 李小龍 ; born Lee Jun-fan, 李振藩)
November 27, 1940 - July 20, 1973 Bio

Bruce lee was the founder of Jeet Kune Do, a hybrid martial arts philosophy drawing from different combat disciplines that is often credited with paving the way for modern mixed martial arts (MMA). Lee is considered by critics, media, and other martial artists to be the most influential martial artist of all time and a pop culture icon of the 20th century, who bridged the gap between East and West. He is credited with promoting Hong Kong action cinema and helping to change the way Asians were presented in American films.

Born in San Francisco and raised in British Hong Kong, Lee was introduced to the Hong Kong film industry as a child actor by his father. However these were not martial art films. His early martial arts experience included Wing Chun (trained under Yip Man), tai chi, boxing (winning a Hong Kong boxing tournament), and apparently frequent street fighting (neighbourhood and rooftop fights). In 1959, Lee, having U.S. citizenship due to his birth, was able to move to Seattle. In 1961, he enrolled in the University of Washington. It was during this time in the United States that he began considering making money by teaching martial arts even though he aspired to an acting career. He opened his first martial arts school, operated out of home in Seattle. After later adding a second school in Oakland, California, he once drew significant attention at the 1964 Long Beach International Karate Championships of California by making demonstrations and speaking. He subsequently moved to Los Angeles to teach, where his students included Chuck Norris, Sharon Tate, and Kareem Abdul-Jabbar. In the 1970s, his Hong Kong and Hollywood-produced films elevated the Hong Kong martial arts films to a new level of popularity and acclaim, sparking a surge of Western interest in Chinese martial arts. The direction and tone of his films dramatically influenced and changed martial arts and martial arts films worldwide.

He is noted for his roles in five feature-length Hong Kong martial arts films in the early 1970s: Lo Wei's The Big Boss (1971) and Fist of Fury (1972); Golden Harvest's Way of the Dragon (1972), directed and written by Lee; and Golden Harvest and Warner Brothers' Enter the Dragon (1973) and The Game of Death (1978), both directed by Robert Clouse.[6] Lee became an iconic figure known throughout the world, particularly among the Chinese, based upon his portrayal of Chinese nationalism in his films,[7] and among Asian Americans for defying Asian stereotypes.[8] Having initially learnt Wing Chun, tai chi, boxing, and street fighting, he combined them with other influences from various sources into the spirit of his personal martial arts philosophy, which he dubbed Jeet Kune Do (The Way of the Intercepting Fist).

Lee died on July 20, 1973, at the age of 32. Since his death, Lee has continued to be a prominent influence on modern combat sports, including judo, karate, mixed martial arts, and boxing, as well as modern popular culture, including film, television, comics, animation and video games. Time named Lee one of the 100 most important people of the 20th century.
EVERY PHOTO SHOWS AN EMOTION

Bruce Lee
Bruce Lee was a martial arts icon, who looms so large in pop culture that the mundane details of his life read like a rare treat. Bruce has been re-invented in a number of ways in the past few years In Cinemax's "Warrior", as the protagonist of his own television concept, in "Ip Man 4": The Finale, as a youthful kung Fu practitioner breaking the traditional barriers. And more infamously, in Quentin Tarrantino's, "Once Upon a Time in Hollywood" as a jive-talking character. His life was to be examined in ESPN "30 for 30" documentary "Be Water" a harrowing documentary chronicling his life, and after being rejected from Hollywood he returned to his parents homeland where he would complete four iconic films in just two years, before passing he would leave an uncompleted project "The Game of Death" that has recently been re-edited by film maker Alan Canvan, offering the audience the most complete cut, turning it from the end reel of an unfinished movie to a thirty minute Art-house film.
Bruce Lee left another great legacy, Thousands of photographs that would capture him in almost every part of his life. Albeit filming in front of the camera, off set, greeting people, being interviewed, clowning around, with his wife and children that he adored or just random candid snaps. For me as I look at the many pictures taken, we see almost a different emotion; His face is one of many expressions that we rarely see even amongst the finest actors of stage and film.

I have compiled a selection of various shots that hopefully capture just a few of the moments during his short but successful life.

This is Bruce "Captured on Camera" Volume one.

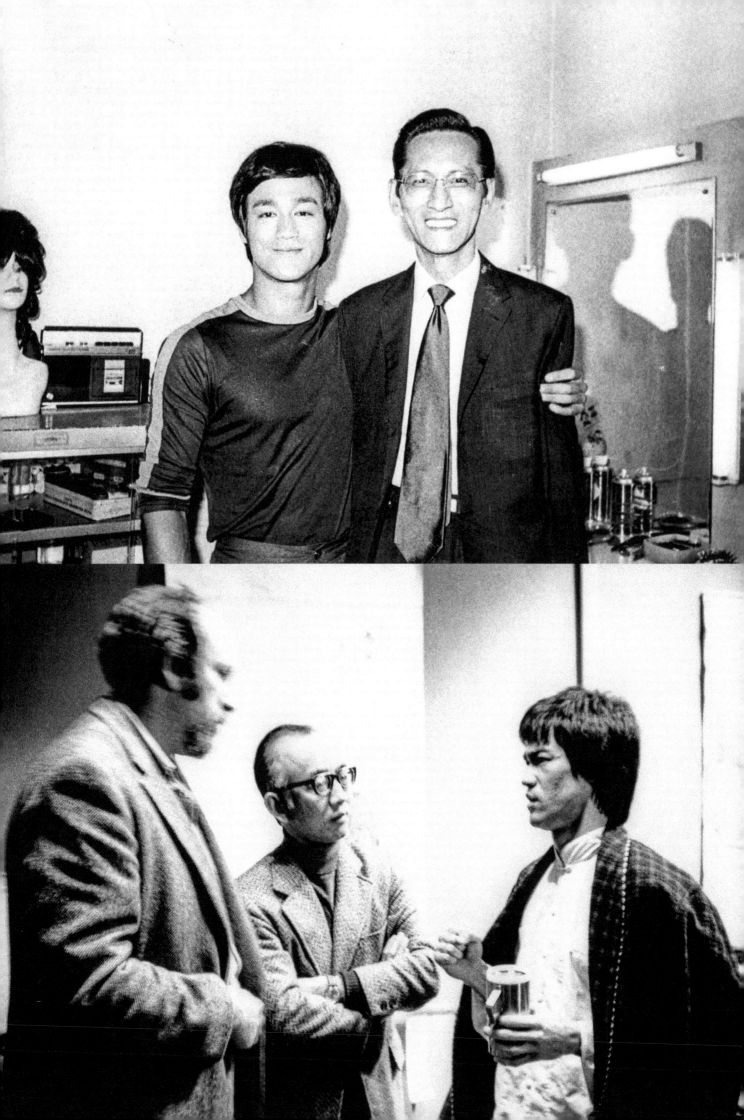

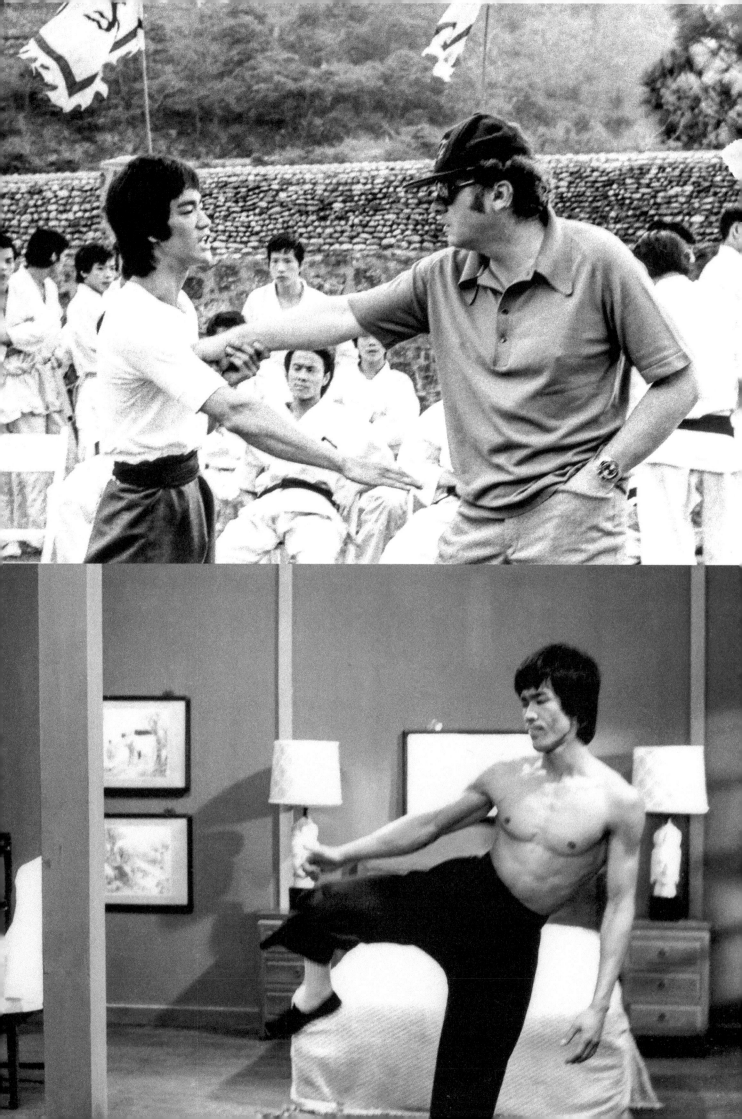

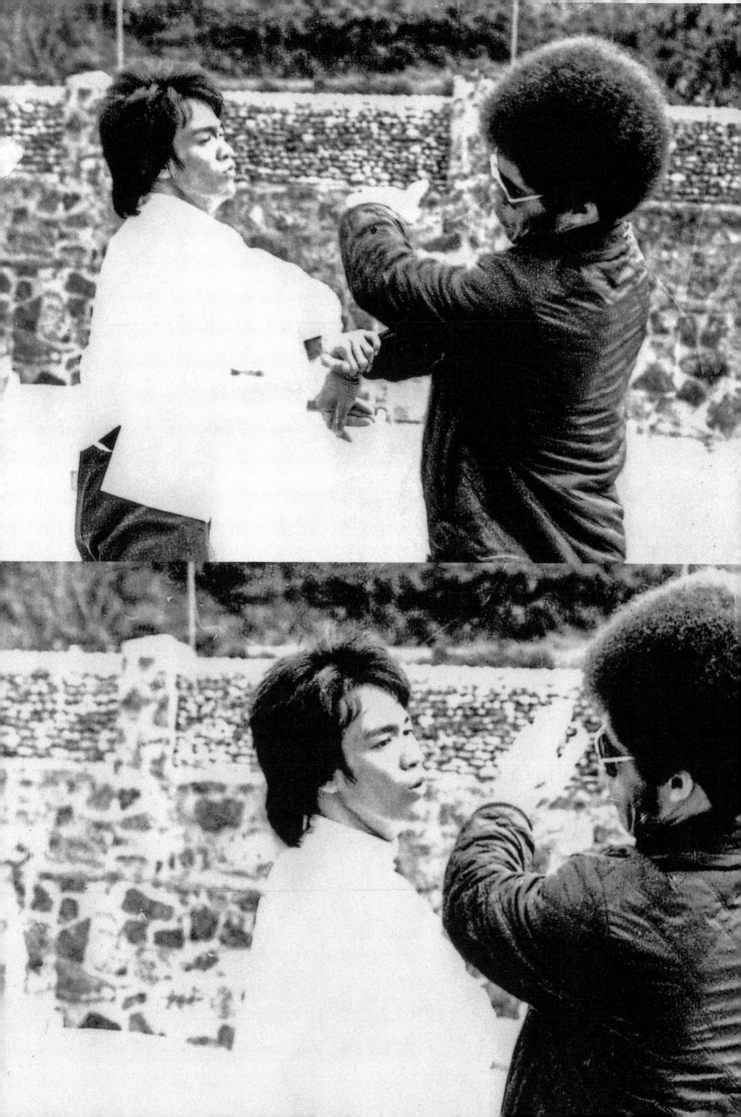

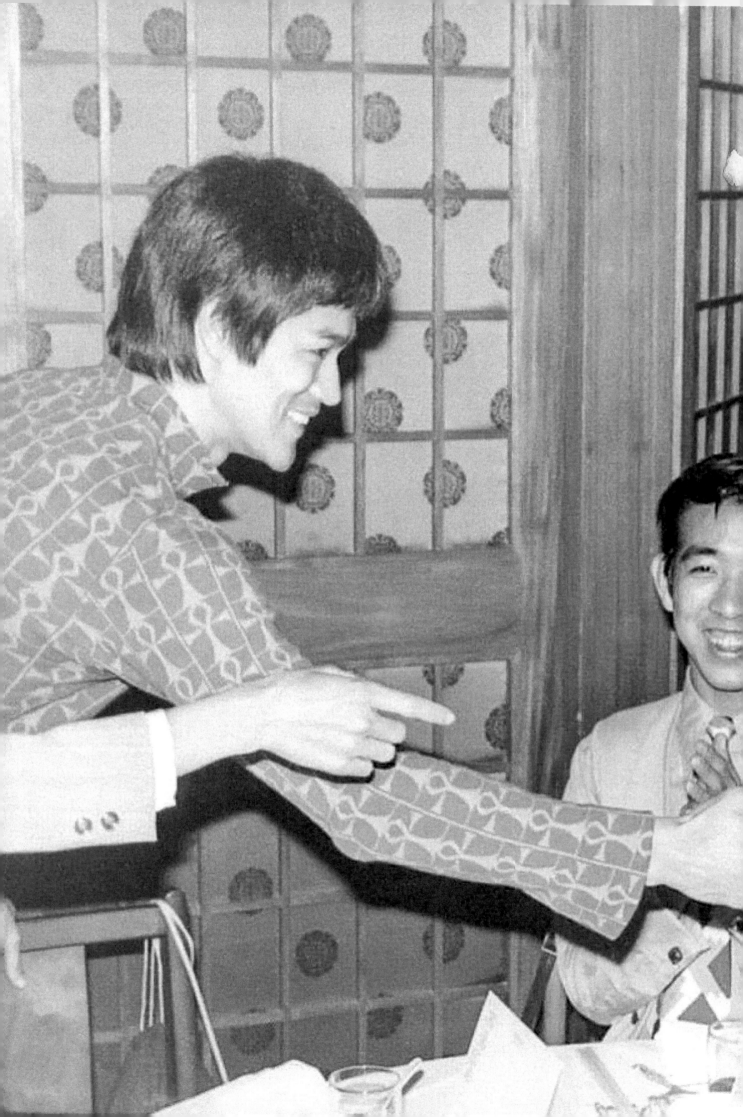

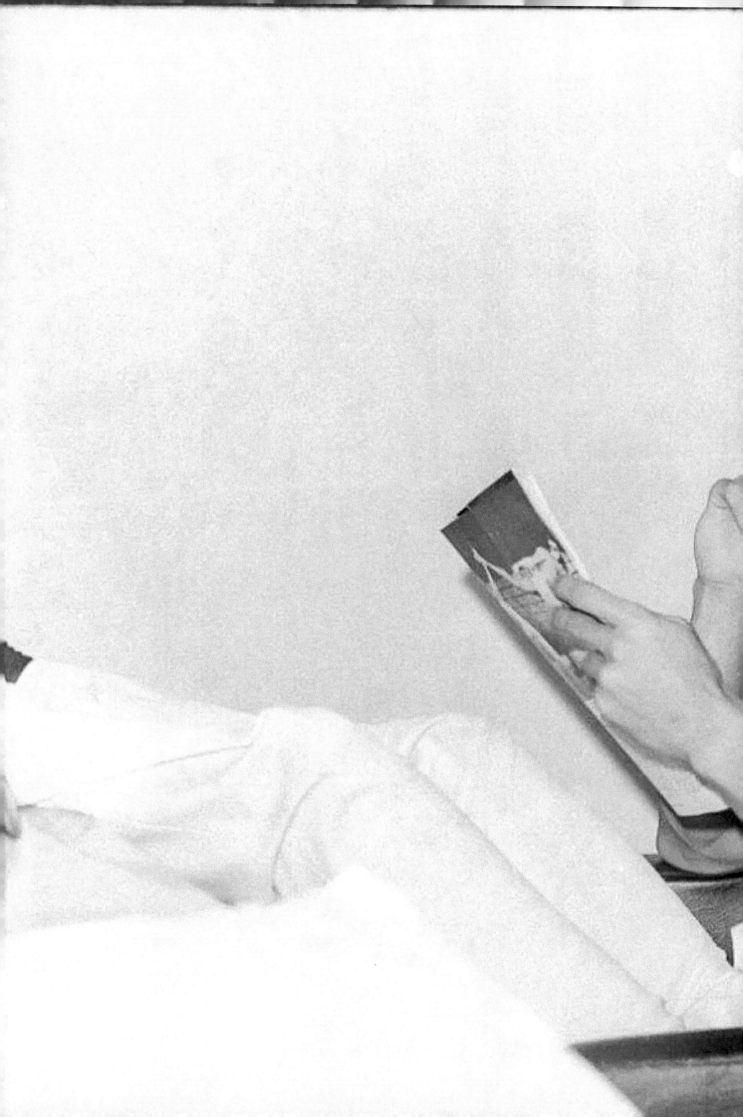

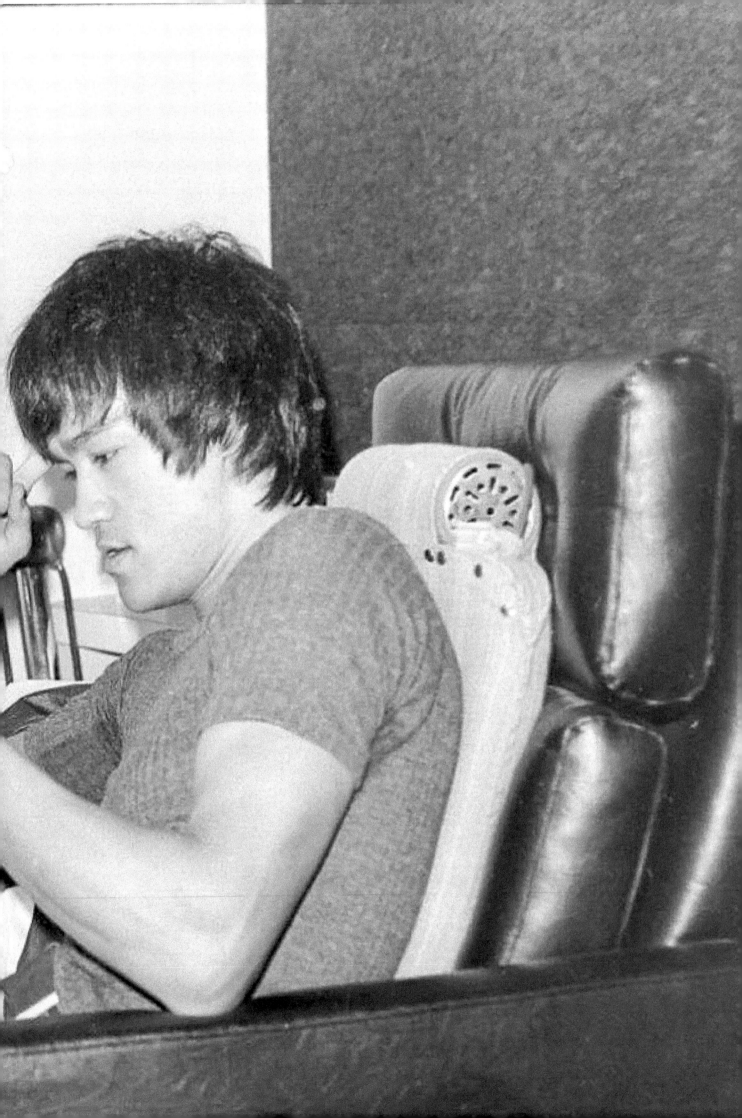

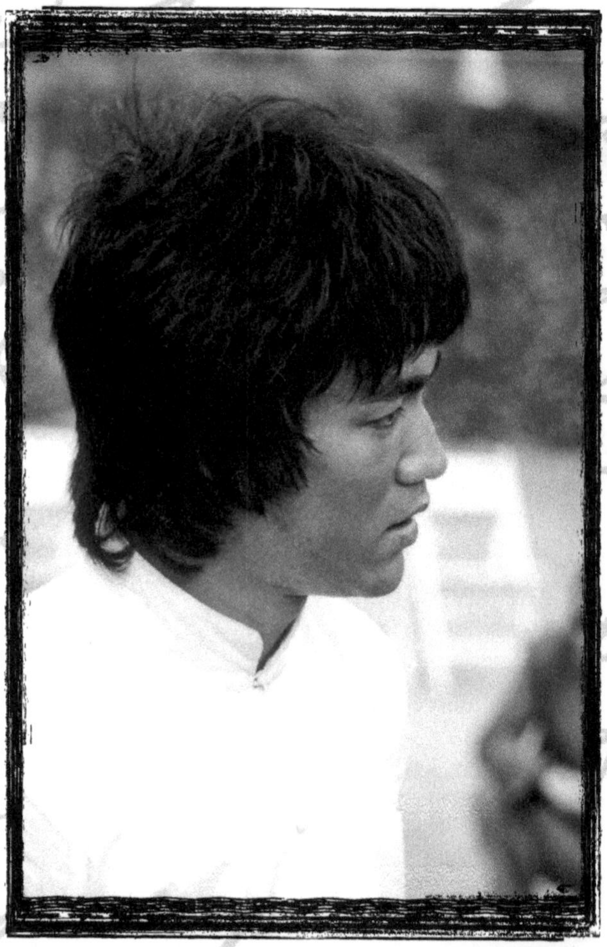
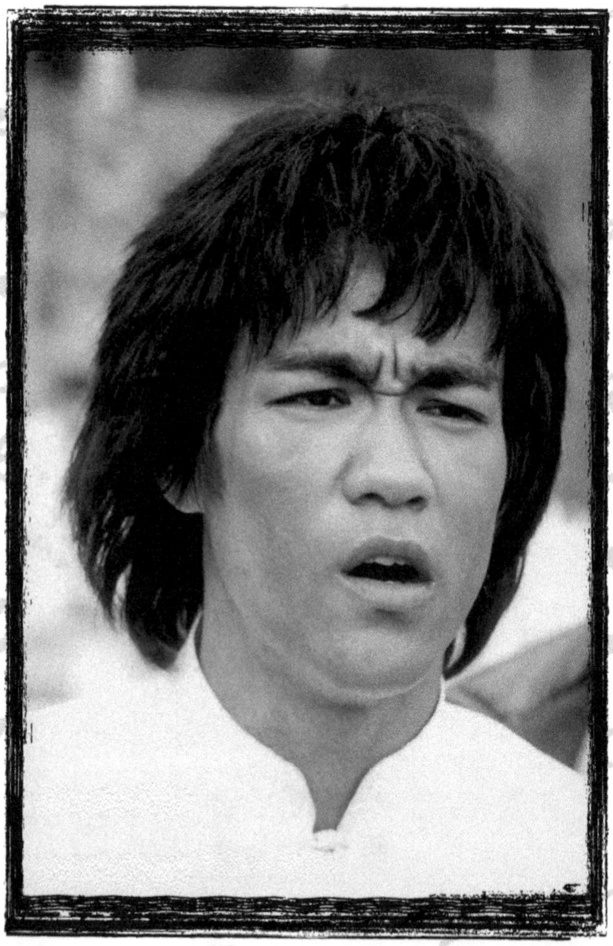
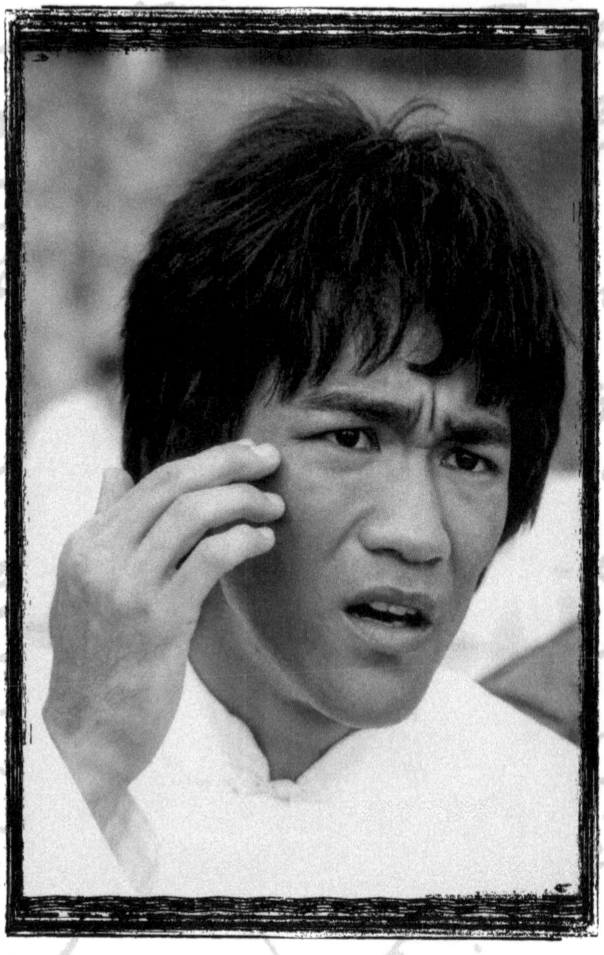
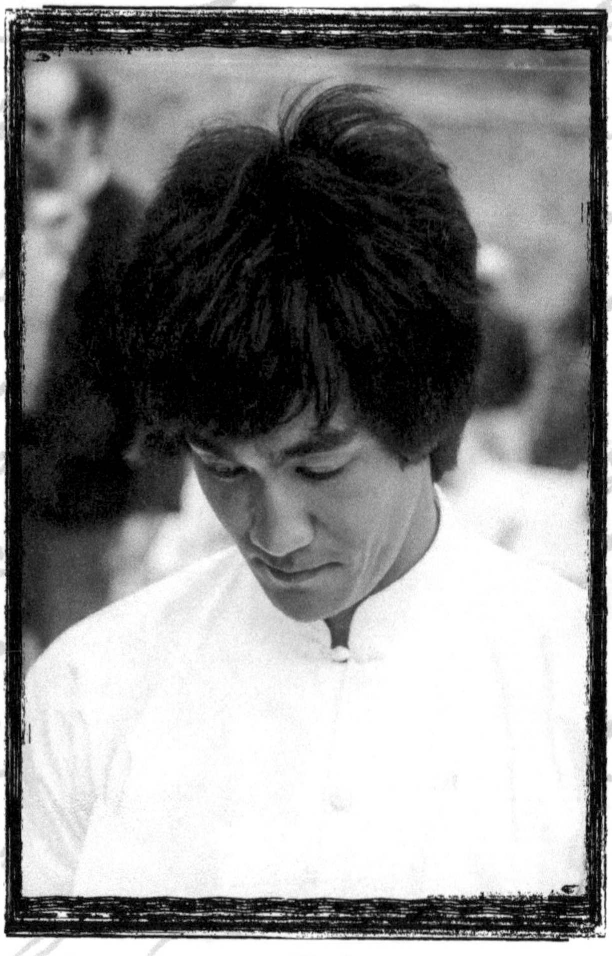

.